Donated by

SAN RAMON LIBRARY FOUNDATION
100 Montgomery • San Ramon • California 94583

AWESOME
SNOWBOARD
Tricks & Stunts

WITHDRAWN

by Lori Polydoros

Reading Consultant:
Barbara J. Fox
Reading Specialist
North Carolina State University

Content Consultants:

Drew Mearns
Executive Director
Action Sports Alliance

Mimi Knoop
Co-Founder
Action Sports Alliance

CAPSTONE PRESS
a capstone imprint

Blazers is published by Capstone Press,
151 Good Counsel Drive, P.O. Box 669, Mankato, Minnesota 56002.
www.capstonepub.com

Books published by Capstone Press are manufactured with paper
containing at least 10 percent post-consumer waste.

Library of Congress Cataloging-in-Publication Data
Polydoros, Lori, 1968–
  Awesome snowboard tricks and stunts / by Lori Polydoros.
    p. cm.—(Blazers. Big air)
  Includes bibliographical references and index.
  Summary: "Describes extreme big-air stunts and tricks performed by professional
snowboarders"—Provided by publisher.
  ISBN 978-1-4296-5412-8 (library binding)
1. Snowboarders. I. Title.
GV857.S57P65 2011
796.93'9—dc22   2010032199

Editorial Credits
Aaron Sautter, editor; Tracy Davies and Kyle Grenz, designers;
    Eric Manske, production specialist

Photo Credits
Alamy/Chris McLennan, 16–17
AP Images, 25
Corbis/Bo Bridges, 6, 10, 23; Reuters/Andy Clark, 13
David Blazek/Burton European Open, 26–27
Getty Images Inc./Brian Bahr, 20; Jed Jacobsohn, cover, 5, 9; Mike Powell, 14–15
Newscom/Wu Wei, 29
Shutterstock/Brian Finestone, 19

Artistic Effects
iStockphoto/Guillermo Perales, peter zelei, 4x6

Printed in the United States of America in Stevens Point, Wisconsin.
092010   005934WZS11

TABLE OF CONTENTS

BIG AIR OVER SNOW

The best pro snowboarders pull off the craziest tricks. They twist and fly off **half-pipes**. They flip and spin while soaring high into the sky. They like to thrill fans with the most amazing stunts.

4

half-pipe—a U-shaped ramp with high walls

5

FACT:
Some people ride regular stance. They keep their left foot forward. Others ride goofy stance. They keep their right foot forward.

50-50 GRIND

In a 50-50 Grind, the snowboarder first does an **ollie** to reach the rail. He then grinds the board across the rail's top. He balances his board without falling over. Then he straightens out before leaping into the snow.

ollie—a trick in which the rider pops the board into the air with his or her feet

INDY GRAB

The **Indy** Grab takes guts. The rider flies into the air and pulls her knees to her chest. She grabs the board **toeside**. In a flash, she straightens her body to stick the landing.

indy—when a rider grabs the toeside of the board with the back hand

toeside—the edge of the board in front of the rider's toes

FACT:
Many snowboard tricks are created from skateboard tricks. Skateboarder Duane Peters invented the Indy Grab in the 1970s.

ALLEY-OOP TAIL GRAB

It's the last run of the day. The rider flies up the ramp at an angle. In the air, he twists and grabs the tail of the board. He spins a half-circle before landing. The Alley-Oop Tail Grab rockets him into first place!

FACT:
Snow parks are full of ramps, jumps, and railings. The obstacles give riders many ways to perform extreme tricks.

Melon 360

Snowboarders do **aerials**, spins, and grabs all at once. For the **Melon 360**, a rider launches off the jump. She reaches behind her back leg to do a melon grab. She spins a full circle as the fans cheer her on.

aerial—a trick performed while in the air

melon—when a rider grabs the heelside of the board with the leading hand

FRONT FLIP

Front flips look easy, but they take a lot of skill. The rider springs the nose of the board off the ramp edge. He throws his weight forward to flip through the air. He lands with a thud and the crowd goes wild!

FACT:
Some top riders can do double front flips.
A few even do triple front flips off cliffs!

torino 2006

15

BACKFLIP

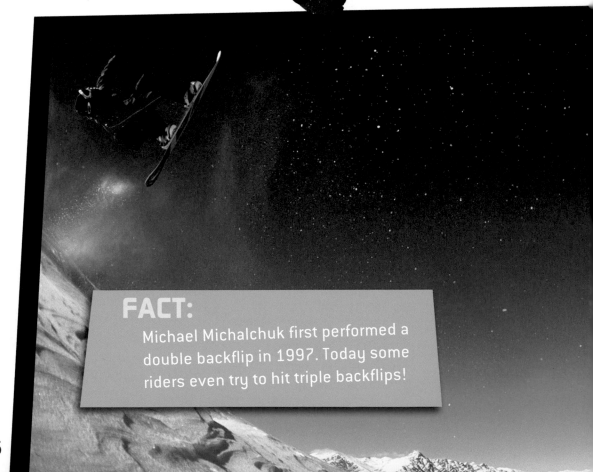

FACT:
Michael Michalchuk first performed a double backflip in 1997. Today some riders even try to hit triple backflips!

Snowboarders need plenty of space for backflips. The rider launches into the sky. He grabs the board and spins backward. While upside down, he finds his landing spot. The snow crunches as he nails a perfect landing!

540 McTwist

A rider launches off the ramp and grabs the board **mute**. In the 540 McTwist, he does a full head-over-heels flip. At the same time, he spins a half-circle. He's like an acrobat tumbling in the air.

FACT:
In 1998 Shannon Dunn-Downing became the first U.S. woman to win an Olympic gold medal in snowboarding.

mute—when a rider grabs the toeside of the board with the front hand

19

720

At the Winter X Games, one rider goes for a 720. He flies off the ramp and grabs the board indy. He stretches out his other arm for extra style points. He does two full spins and then sticks the landing!

LIEN RODEO

The rider flies off the ramp frontside. He spins head over heels for a backward flip. At the same time, he grabs the board and spins a half-circle. The snow crunches as he makes a perfect landing. He's just pulled off a great Lien **Rodeo**!

rodeo—a combination of a flip and a sideways spin

BRODEO

It's the last rider's turn at the Winter X Games. The boarder does a backside flip and spins while grabbing indy. The awesome Backside Rodeo Flip, or Brodeo, helps him win the gold medal!

FACT:
A superpipe is a half-pipe with walls at least 18 feet (5.5 meters) tall.

DOUBLE CORK 1080

The Double Cork 1080 is an amazing and dangerous trick. In this crazy stunt, a boarder does two full flips in the air. At the last second, he twists around to stick the landing. It totals three full spins of wild flight!

FACT:
Pro boarder David Benedek first pulled off the Double Cork trick in 2006.

THE TOMAHAWK

Shaun White created the stunning Tomahawk trick. He flies off the ramp and does two forward flips. At the same time, he also does one-and-a-half sideways spins. Then he lands smoothly on the snow. The fans go wild for the breathtaking stunt!

FACT:
Shaun White has won two Olympic gold medals in snowboarding. He also holds a record nine gold medals for snowboarding at the Winter X Games.

GLOSSARY

aerial (AIR-ee-uhl)—any trick performed while the rider is in the air

half-pipe (HAF-pipe)—a U-shaped ramp with high walls

indy (IN-dee)—a grab in which the rider places his or her back hand on the toeside of the board

melon (MEL-uhn)—a grab in which the rider places his or her leading hand on the heelside of the board

mute (MYOOT)—a grab in which the rider places his or her leading hand on the toeside of the board

ollie (OL-ee)—a move where the rider pops the board into the air with his or her feet

rodeo (ROH-dee-oh)—a trick that combines a flip with a sideways spin

toeside (TOH-side)—the edge of the board in front of the rider's toes

READ MORE

Gitlin, Marty. *Shaun White: Snow and Skateboard Champion.* Berkeley Heights, N.J.: Enslow Publishers, Inc., 2009.

Mason, Paul. *Snowboarding : The World's Most Sizzling Snowboard Spots and Techniques.* Passport to World Sports. Mankato, Minn.: Capstone Press, 2011.

O'Neal, Claire. *Extreme Snowboarding with Lindsey Jacobellis.* Hockessin, Del.: Mitchell Lane Publishers, 2009.

INTERNET SITES

FactHound offers a safe, fun way to find Internet sites related to this book. All of the sites on FactHound have been researched by our staff.

Here's all you do:

Visit *www.facthound.com*

Type in this code: 9781429654128

Super-cool stuff!

Check out projects, games and lots more at
www.capstonekids.com

INDEX